Vent

By Rosalyn Alexandra

Rosalyn Alexandra
rosalynalexandrapoetry@gmail.com

Author: Rosalyn Alexandra
Illustrator: Rosalyn Alexandra
Publisher: Rosalyn Alexandra

ISBN: 978-0-578-46830-3 (Paperback)

First Edition
10 9 8 7 6 5 4 3 2 1

Vent

a letter to you

Dear,

Some of you know me personally whereas others don't know me at all. Which is okay because through my words all of you will grow to truly know a part of me by the end of this. It's scary feeling like a stranger to people who know my name. It's terrifying opening your heart to people who know nothing about you- other than what you tell them. Who I am as a person is just an idea in your mind. The impression I leave justifies who you think I am and always will. I don't know who you are, but I've written about you. I may not know your name, or your favorite color, or the way your hair frames your face just right, but I know you hear the echo of your name through my words. You may cry, you may get chills, you may throw my book, you might stare at the pages blankly, you could smile, feel warm inside, you might feel something. Feeling is what this book is about. It's natural and human to feel. You may feel things you're not ready to embrace or that you've been ignoring in your heart. Let me tell you one thing I've learned from spending two years writing this book. There is no right time to feel things. We experience so many different emotions every day and waiting for the right time to express your heart is not real because feelings fade and change. Letting them out, you learn from yourself. Venting is healthy. Venting is what helps me breathe when I suffocate myself with emotions. Take this book, take my words, take my heart and learn from the words I've patched together. Heartbreak and falling in love and betrayal and laughter all these feelings that lead from tears to blushing are natural. I hope the words I've sewn together help you. I hope you feel understood. I am you. Because without you there is no meaning behind my words. And without you, I am just black ink on paper.

Happy tears,

r.a.

The states of my mind are yours to explore.
Take a trip down memory lane
and swim in the depths of my soul.
Sail the beats of my heart
And drive in circles around the boulevard of my thoughts.
I'm yours to explore, just take my hand.
We'll take a stand by journeying this world without a plan.
So, follow me, let's runaway to be

Free

Though,
I may be writing in black ink,
I hope my words are in such vibrant color
that the colors of my love
draw a home in the
chambers of your heart.

This bleak world lives in a spectre of black and white array. There's no depth or dimension within our thoughts because a dull world consists of dull people. We move with a grey robotic line of sight. We go for what's necessary not what we want because there is nothing desirable in a world of similarities. Although, there is always an exception. The world may be black and white, but black is a concept. Colors combine to create some of the darkest shades. How is it, in a black and white world, I stumble upon the most captivating shade of them all when they all look the same? The colors within you are blended in such a way even the brightest of stars are not pressured to shine so bright. They lie comfortably within you. In this faded value of black and white, you have struck me like a white crayon coloring on black paper. You make people feel like they can make a difference in the darkest of times. I have fallen in love with the words you speak, the things you've experienced, and you as a whole. It makes you who you are. The different shades of color you're made of are an artist's drug because only nature can produce such a natural feeling.

You're so peculiar.
You don't protect yourself with an umbrella.
You don't warm yourself with a yellow rain slicker,
even though I insist you do
because I don't want you to get sick.
No, you twirl in the blue and splash in my puddles
dancing in the rain while everyone runs for cover.

You burn yourself
to keep others warm.
If you ever find yourself growing cold,
I will do what I can to spark hope
back into your eyes.

"Your hands are beautiful
You have the hands of kindness."

The smile in your eyes
is a vibrant ray of light
beaming across a dimly lit town.

There's no point
in locking your heart away in a storage.
No matter how big the lock is,
someone will eventually try to pick it.

To me,

Loving you is natural and obvious.
I hope one day you feel the same about

Yourself.

1018 DRIVE
July
10
2003
MO

7

I gave you the wheel to drive under the night sky
We drove for hours and hours surfing the coastline
The radio blasted and our voices rang
But our voices were no match for how bright your eyes sang.
We danced and laughed as I looked at our map
No real destination I just need your hand and a nap
We don't sleep very much just continue to drive
It's what keeps the adventure alive.
You give me one look and I can feel the nostalgia
"I know, I should've called ya."
We stop by a gas station and raid the junk food aisle
We ran to the car and, as I grabbed my seatbelt, I stole a smile.
You put your hand over the belt and assured me to let go
I smirked and I did because with you I just know.
We drove through the night
I had no seat belt, it wasn't tight
I felt free- finally, nothing holding us back
No sorrow or anger; my heart without a crack
You remind me life doesn't need a designated stop
And that sometimes all you need is a cold pop
I was never much for travel until I met you
I never deemed it necessary to leave for a moment or two
But you took me by surprise
With your warm and kind eyes
You showed me what it was like to live
And reminded me what it was like to give
Such a pure soul like yours I wish to hold
I would show you to the world and yell "Behold"
But, darling, the world doesn't deserve to see
The person you can and will be.

I wish people could see you the way I see you, little honey bee.

You drift and bob up and down through a sea of golden fields as the sun starts to rise and wake up the wind and sky.

You dance from flower to flower gently greeting the roses and passing by honey suckle groves. "You've always been fond of such a sweet dulcet aroma." You ride the breeze to a garden where you find yourself spreading yellow everywhere. "You've always been fond of yellow. You deemed it a color of innocence and childlike nature." Others see it as a danger. People swing at you and scream in terror as you dart by them. Your soft textures are masked by your bitter sting that shadows and follows your every move. People choose to acknowledge the threat that you could be rather than your true stripes. To them, it's easier to fear you than to understand you. There's nothing to be ashamed of, little honeybee. They don't know it kills you to sting them, but you must continue spreading the yellow

even if it's at the cost of others.

When you told me the truth,
when you handed me your heart,
when you cried on my shoulder,
you may think you're being weak,
or that you are unlovable.
You may think I see you differently,
but you haven't changed my view,
just added a little more.
And I fell a little more each time.

To see the world through
your eyes would be a lovely opportunity.
You see in such color even grey bleeds red.
Sadly, when you gaze into your reflection
you cannot see the depths of your soul.
If only you could peer through my glasses
so, you could see the paint God
used to stroke your eyes.

The act of giving flowers
to the ones we love
could be seen as generic,
but the flowers themselves
don't conform.
So elegant and graceful.
You're a flower.
You should be shared with all,
but you are kept for someone special.

I am no pianist, but when you look at me,
I can feel the rhythm of my heart composing symphonies.
The light in your eyes dances to the sound of our laughter.
You know the song of my soul
And wrote some of the lyrics of my life.

I never took right turns in my life.
You were always my left turn,
but I didn't mind taking the long way
about things if I walked with you.

A flower in the morning,
A note by your side,
A song on the piano,
A night you need a ride,
A call which leads to snoring,
A smile that takes me high,
A look that gives me fireworks
I wish I could deny.
You're the fuel behind my hand,
The reason I take a stand,
The moon is in your eyes,
They always take me by surprise.
They tell me I don't have to hold,
They encourage me to unfold
The dog-eared map of my soul.

I thought I found a home in college with my sorority sisters,
but I stepped out of line and they kicked me out.
I felt trapped.
That's okay, a home should allow me to stand for a cause.

I thought I found a home with a friend in an apartment downtown,
but she brought too many strangers home.
I felt invaded.
That's okay, a home shouldn't make you feel uncomfortable in your own bed.

I thought I found a home when I pulled up to my parents' driveway,
but my dad chased me out with a beer bottle in hand.
I felt lethargic.
That's okay, a home shouldn't flood my mind with monsters I drew on
sidewalks when I was a kid.

Now I remember why I left.

I parked my car on the side of a back road a couple miles from a small town
with big ghosts.
I sat on the curb with my head in hand. I reached for my phone and looked
through my contacts. A pit of helplessness sunk in my stomach as I realized I
didn't know who to call. I looked to the sky and the stars shined so bright
and danced through the air to keep me company, but I felt as if they were
taunting me.
I set my phone down and let the tears prance from my cheeks to the ground.

"Come home," you whispered, "I have tissues."

I drove about two miles into your arms.

I knew I found a home when you wrapped your arms
around me and the rays of your smile welcomed the
morning's sun.

The boogie man knew me by name. He lived in the closet in the back of my head. He liked to lure me in the dark and introduce me to the voices that kept him company. I was afraid of them and I'm not sure why. Maybe, it's because they've told me the truth and it's hard to face it so I would rather fear it. Crazy thing was, you were friends with the boogie man. You made him look like a man with a soul rather than a monster. You often make me feel the same way. Reminding me that I'm just another girl in this world looking to the night sky hoping to forget why she was crying.

"May I borrow a rose from your lawn
For the girl I loved at dawn?"

There was something
exceptionally
beautiful
about you today.
You've always
been lovely,
but I think
I saw genuine bliss
in your eyes for the first time.

You know,
I know plenty of things
like how to recite my ABC's
and how to count past one hundred.
Although, there's one thing
I can't quite put my finger on.
My heart reacts to the thought of you
with these inexplicable emotions.
I think this is the first time
I don't mind not knowing the answers.

If we're both contradictions
we contradict each other
to the point we are one;
we finish each other.

Would it be a cliché
to hate roses because roses are clichés?
I feel like I would give up on this vendetta
against the flower if you were to bend down
on one knee with a single rose in your hand.
I think running away together is rather general too,
but I'd do it in a heartbeat with you.

Small town drives,
Where time is frozen and no one is alive,
Lead to adventures.
It was my favorite kind of weather,
The kind
When the wind coos and the sun doesn't leave us blind.
The leaves crunched under our feet as we hiked.
The only thing we cold hear was a synchronized heartbeat.
I held your hand
Just in case because falling wasn't part of the plan.
But I fell anyways
And you caught me in a daze.
I think in that moment, I fell for you
As I looked into your sea of blue.
I thought you were going to kiss me.
In fact, you could've taken advantage of the opportunity.
Rather, you looked to the ground,
And let your hair fall to your eyes and walked me around.
We talked for hours on end often getting sidetracked
And laughing as we returned back
To your car.
We sang and drove, and your heart went ajar.
You talked about your feelings
And all of your personal dealings
As we passed by cars and buildings, I couldn't help
But realize what I had felt.
Your words surprised me
They often set me free
They help me let
Go of some things I never could quite forget,
Until I'm with you
I feel content and true
Like the way eyes smile
Or the realization I'm not a piled
Up mess.
I can't help but feel like a girl wearing a dress
On a lovely night outing
Nothing leaving me doubting
about these feelings for you
that will hopefully follow through.

If this is what falling in love feels like
I don't want to be caught.

I can see the look in your eyes,
you want my heart.
It's silly of you to think that
you don't already have it.

I am a musician. I can learn chords and rhythms with the flick of my wrist. Give me a song and I'll learn and memorize it for anyone. When it comes to you, I find myself crying until I fall asleep thinking of the right lyrics to get you to fall for me. Wondering if you'll love me or things I do.

Sometimes, when you look at me,
I feel the need to cry for your eyes are so captivating.
I mustn't blink for I fear if I look away
from your gaze for even just a second,
I would lose our connection.

It's weird to think we are someone's last thought before we go to bed.

It's strange to think we are someone's favorite greeting.

It's peculiar to think we may be someone's reason to keep breathing.

It's ironic the person we want the most will never see us in the ways we want to be seen until it's too late.

How weird it is of us to love the people who don't want us.

Clouds bustle and crowd the sky like the thoughts in my head that cloud my judgment. The warm haze radiating behind the clouds paints color over my pale cheeks. My chapped lips remind me of all the times my constant gnawing stopped me from saying what's on my mind. I feel my eyes glaze over as I stare at the horizon. I hoped that you'd come up behind me, rest your hand on my shoulder, and sit next to me. Instead, I am accompanied by the whispers of the green glade and the patter of rocks ricocheting across the ground, tossed to the side. Maybe I sit here and watch the world move about to escape the world inside my mind. I often find myself making up another reality where the clouds are the ground we stand on and grass decorates the sky. Sure, it sounds silly, but in this world, I was meant for you and you were meant for me. You are there, but you're not here. I find myself mixing what I want with what I have, and this is dangerous because here I am yours, but you are not mine

A kiss is the last thing I can give you.

The last chance to show you what I feel.

It's the only thing that can express the words that won't roll off my lips.

I gave you my heart, my soul, and my mind.

The most intimate part of my body so soft and pure.

My lips have been cut and they've bled.

I've been hit many times for not keeping my trap shut.

The words I can't say that come from my hand long to tell you how they feel.

I look at you and I see a star, so bright in the night sky. You're seen by everyone, yet too far away to touch. You mesmerize and capture people. Hell, people even wish on you. You can bring so much hope, but you only show up at night and then you go away the next day. I wished on you at 11:11 hoping tomorrow would be different. Maybe you'd still be here when I woke, but you weren't. You take what you need at night and shine on other crowds during my day. I'm just another wish to you. I'm not even your wish, yet you were mine all along.

I could have kissed you that night. We gazed at the stars the air was right. Music played in the distance as we laughed. Something about your lips looked nostalgic as if my lips and yours were old friends. I laid beside you keeping at a safe distance. I always feared you would flinch if I grazed your arm. God, how could I ever have the audacity to kiss you? Instead, I listened to the breeze and the distant call of airplanes trailing the sky. I heard your heartbeat that night. It was timid yet present. I think our heartbeats kissed yet our bodies strayed away as we laid under the moon. If I had kissed you that night, I fear I would have lost your heart, but, if I had kissed you, maybe I would still feel mine.

I sat on a bench as the sun kissed my tears
Hoping to feel cared for since you couldn't hold the bear
The tears soaked back into my cheeks as they decorated my face
I couldn't help but feel my heart get put into place
But when I see you again, I know it'll shatter more
I dunno about you, but I can't help but hold the door

Love's a tricky thing I thought we caught it together, but
Love flew away and left us cold with one single feather
Who are we to think we captured Love?

Love is wild, Love is free
Not angry and chilling leaving parts of us in debris

I sat under the stars hoping to feel you looking too
But as I sat on the ground the stars told me the truth
In the middle of the night, thoughts screaming in my head
Do you feel this way too? Or are you sound asleep in your bed?
Seeing your picture on my wall makes my heart take a leap
Too bad I wasn't yours to keep

Love's a tricky thing I thought we caught it together, but
Love flew away and left us cold with one single feather
Who are we to think we captured Love?

Love is wild, Love is free
Not angry and chilling leaving parts of us in debris

So, I sat down thinking for days on end
Stories and theories on loop no one would quite comprehend but
Despite the thoughts and time spent through wonder
I couldn't help but sit in the rain and listen to the thunder
Time has a way of repeating
Might you remember? I can still feel my heart beating
And like the trees love the sun
The sun goes away, and the moon will always be there when it's
done

Like I said

Love's a tricky thing I thought we caught it together, but
Love flew away and left us cold with one single feather
Who are we to think we captured Love?

Love is wild, Love is free
Not angry and chilling leaving parts of us in debris

I'm not quite sure why I'm crying anymore.
Everything is so blurred together
like the mascara smears on my cheeks
blending in with my dark circles from all
of those restless nights.

If I were to rip open my heart,
a bundle of butterflies would flutter out
and would release this storm inside my chest.
You caused the earthquake inside
to tear down homes and spread despair.

-Butterfly Effect

I loved so hard
I broke my heart.
I'm sorry I spilled it all over
you.

The smell of you lingers on my sweater and tricks my brain into thinking you're still here. Oh, how I wish I could still hear the echo of your heartbeat. The very thought makes my lip quiver and my body begin to shake. If only these arms wrapped around my waist were yours so I could pull you closer and our bodies would mold into one shape.

I keep finding myself coming back to you
like the shadow connected to your feet.
It's fun when the sun comes out to play
and we chase the butterflies in the day.
But it's sad when I fade into darkness
when the moon comes over the day.

If I was her,
Maybe it would be different.

A party danced in my mind. I celebrated all of my successes and failures and danced the night away in my bedroom. I felt on top of the world. You joined this party of one and we collided. I felt the love you had for me as we connected and intertwined our souls making my heart soar high. I started to float to the heavens. I was so high you had to tie a string around me to keep me somewhat grounded. It was 10:47 P.M. when the music stopped, but I was still dancing on my own. You touched my hand and sat me down. I looked at you as you grabbed your coat. You glanced at the door then dropped your eyes to the floor. I started to lose my high and sink. You broke the news to me and left me to pick up the broken glasses from the spilled champagne.

I can taste the sorrow of last night's grief from the dry streaks of haunting tears and distant memories. The night old and frail dying to bore dawn. I lie in the grass looking towards the stars hoping to join them one day not knowing you'd beat me to it. I stand on my toes and reach for you in the sky hoping to get closer, but the more I stretched the farther you seemed. People would say you were the brightest star, but I'd disagree. You aren't a star. People would say you consisted of the darkest parts of the moon but shined enough for the night's creatures to find their ways. I'd disagree. You aren't the moon. You aren't a resonate chill left by a deep sigh from the earth as it blows across a field. Though, you are always present. You aren't an insecure flower crouched and closed from the open air- you never hide your true colors. You've never been the sun. No one ever chased or pawned after you. You just stood in the background.

I'm just a broken record.
I play the same song on rewind,
and the only time she comes to
listen is when she relates to the
lyrics.

I'm pathetic
for ignoring that those quotes
aren't about me,
yet I'm still smiling
as if those words are intended
for me.

The more pages
I seem to add to my story
the more heartbreak left branded
on my heart

My loved ones before you wrote on my heart with a pencil and when they left it made my life easier to erase their marks; so temporary. Sure, my heart still had faded scribbles and light wrinkles left from the eraser, but you could hardly tell. When I ran into you, I looked like a blank canvas. You didn't start with a light sketch. You grabbed a paintbrush and splattered scarlet letters which colored the chambers of my heart. I fell in love with your street art and radicalism. You took a step back and looked at your progress but grew bored of your piece. You left me for another heart to create art out of. I tried to erase your strokes, but the stains stayed. I scrubbed and scratched nothing could remove the damage you left on me. You vandalize hearts because you get too bored creating one lovely masterpiece. You left me incomplete because you'd rather have a multitude of incompletions than one masterpiece.

There's hope back in my eyes because,
maybe, you'll let me love you the way
you should've been loved this whole time.
And maybe, just maybe, you'll love me harder.

This kiss can't be a kiss goodbye
because, if it is, the last butterfly inside
my heart will be free
and I'm not sure it would ever
come back.

My lips throb when I think of you
because it's a reminder
from the words
that left bite marks in my cheeks.
They wanted so badly
to be said
but were left in captivity
as they paced back in forth in my mind.

I can feel the ghost of your fingertips on my arm when your eyes pierce through mine. I see the spirit of memories shadow my favorite places that somehow all lead back to you. When you left, your memory stayed and haunted me through the halls and down the street. The words you said, the things we did all came rushing back to me, the good and bad. It's sad that we don't remember much of the good when it's over because we are so blinded by the pain, or maybe, it's the realization that the person I thought I knew was never truly there, rather a phantom.

My chest began flaring up with this ache
when the door slammed.
The awareness of my heartbeat is surreal.
I feel my heart reminding my body
that it's there. It's bouncing and fluttering
exciting my stomach.
My lungs rattle and shake
as they pull on my heartstrings.
My eyes feel glazed over and bloodshot.
Everything inside me
feels sad and in a
d a z e.

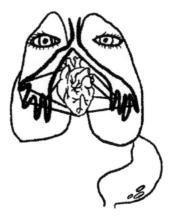

I trembled in your arms
because I feared
you would reject the last part of me
I had to offer.
I was scared
you didn't want the last thing
that made me who I am.
The part of me
that could show you the passion
behind my words and the delicacy of my love.

Sometimes,
I just wanna hold you close
and tell you everything
will be okay,
but I am so afraid to touch you.
I fear if I come too close
you would turn me away
and say that you mistook me for
someone else.

I'll be waiting.
Even when the clock runs out of time
Even when the stars hide their light
When the trees stop standing
And the grass stops growing
I'll be waiting.
Because even when these things stop
I won't stop loving you.

I
keep
feeling like
three days
have passed,
but it's still
today.

A
poem
a day
keeps those
thoughts away

There are two highways that divide my mind:
the logical and the emotional side.
Lord, please help their intersections and the people and thoughts
that were harmed in the car accident last night.

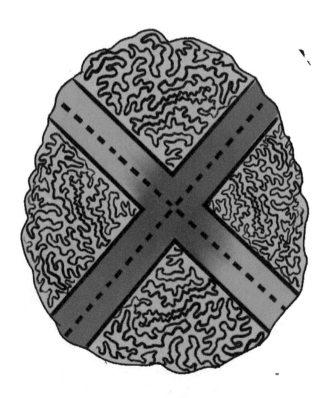

I'm gambling with my heart
and I'm going all in
even though I'm broke right now.

For the longest time,
my heart was an arboretum for all butterflies.
They came from the heart of Mexico
and traveled to the edges of America.
The strings inside me wove together and captured them.

They fluttered and bounced around lightly
like bubbles dancing with the breeze on a spring afternoon.
When the bubbles popped,
they tickled my insides
and brought a smile to my face.

The butterflies pollinate the flowers
you grew last spring.
The ones that bloomed in the summertime.
Red roses popping from the veins encasing my heart.

You touched my heart to pick my roses.
At first, you were careful to touch me
because you were afraid to get hurt.
You were right to be afraid,
but I should've been the one worried.

You pruned my flowers away and cut too deep.
You jabbed at my walls and avoided my thorns for you feared to get cut.
You backed away from my roses, shears in hand.
You tripped over a vein and popped it in the process.

I only bled a little, but the hole was big enough for a butterfly to escape.
Little by little, they started to trickle out
until my garden was abandoned.
Once the butterflies left, there was no one to mend the flowers
of my heart, so they withered away.

Twelve years
down the line,
I promise you
I'll still be the girl
with a bleeding heart.

Remembering
all those nights
and those heartbreaking fights
leave me a bit sad.
I must be mad
to miss nights like those
where we were left exposed.
Out in the light,
you left in such a fright
leaving me alone
with no flesh to protect my bone.

I'm sitting here,
in my bathtub,
listening to the beats of my heart
sink with the water as everything
goes down the drain.

Music can't distract me. I find you hidden in the lyrics I sing. You synchronize with the beats of my heart. If you stop the song, then my heart stops. I'm chained to the rhythm, mesmerized, and enchanted like some moth drawn to a fluorescent light. The closer I get the closer I am to hurting myself. I get burned and I fall to the ground, but I heal my wings and head towards the light again. It doesn't matter how much you hurt me because I am strong enough to pick myself back up but not enough to let you go. You're killing me, yet you're the only thing that's keeping me alive.

I wake up and dance in my room
to an anthem that riots my soul.
I scream and sing dancing
around my feelings that were
spilled across the floor.
I do this to brush the sleep away and
to scare the phantom of you
that torments my nights.

Nothing is happening
and that's the problem.
Nothing is something so light
yet so heavy on the heart.
It weighs you down
like gravity keeps us anchored.
There's no hope for us
to reach the surface.

Why can't I be free of this anxiety?
Since when did butterflies turn into cicadas
in my stomach rattling my bones
and shaking my insides.

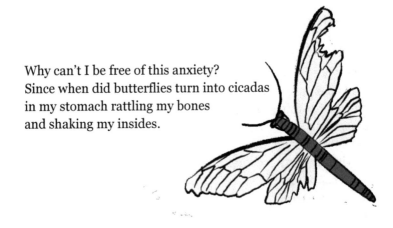

Alcohol tastes bitter
until you have something to drown,
but it's sweet as honey
when you don't want to feel.
I quickly get drained from my emotions
like an alcoholic drains the bar.
It's funny how tears and beer taste the same:
salty and harsh.
I get drunk on heartbreak and it seems
I'm addicted to intoxicating people.
I love how they make me feel,
but I hate the hangover.

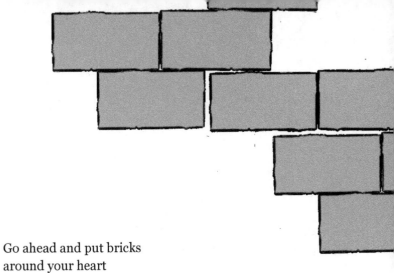

Go ahead and put bricks
around your heart
and wonder why no one
wants to come in.

"I hate you so much
for loving me the way
I should be loved."

-Your Drifting Words

My mind feels
claustrophobic
in this small town.

To feel numb
is to feel too much
of everything.

How does it feel to know
you murdered someone
yet they are still walking?
Stepping closer and closer to you
yet such a distant whisper
sending a chill up your spine.
A presence so strong the hairs
on the back of your neck scream in alarm.
A memory that is long forgotten
yet an image engraved in your mind.
You've been branded as a killer.

Go ahead and barricade the doors and lock the windows of your crumbling castle. You've lost your best fighters. You have no pawns to play. You don't have a king to run away with because, darling, he's on the run from you. I don't know who you're trying to hide from. You create this dragon constructed out of your insecurities and anger and you hide from her. You're waiting for Prince Charming to rescue you, but, in reality, no one can rescue you from the beast inside. You cast yourself away in a place that's about to collapse as if someone you fear is trying to capture you. Dear, there's no one behind those walls. You'll realize this when your little structure falls apart. No one will be waiting for you willing to pick up your pieces because you chased us all away when you detonated your heart of self-destruction.

You lost me
at together,
because,
from what
I understand,
this is
just you.
It has never been about us,
It has always been about you.
So, please,
don't sell me
the idea of us
because you're
just another
conceited cheat.

I don't want an excuse.
I don't want your reasons because, frankly,
they aren't worth my time.
You say your words in a different order every damn time
and expect me not to catch on to your rhythm.
You affect people in so many ways,
but the only thing you make me feel is pity.

My hand hurts
from writing so much.
Then again,
so does my heart
from all the words
you spray painted on
that you didn't mean.

With all these voices inside my head,
I've forgotten which one sounds like mine
until I'm not even me anymore.

I sat at a hotel bar with a cigarette lit between my chapped lips
I've lost the keys to my car
which means I can't get away from the nightmares of my California daydreams
my dress rides up to my thighs
the heels boosted what little confidence I had from my leftover high when I walked past your table
that unfortunate day in late April
I tried to numb the pain with old habits like drinking, dancing, and snorting cocaine
but nothing can kill the throbbing beats of my bleeding heart
I stared at old art and old pictures I drew as a kid
So young and innocent until what you did
I wonder if you see me in the color pink
or do you write about me during late nights with a pen running out of ink?
Do tell me what exactly you say
about that cold April night when you took away my days.

A blind woman can see my soul
better than you ever would.
What does that say about you?

Maybe you told me everything I wanted to hear
to get everything you wanted out of me.
The hero to a broken girl.
The broken ones aren't strong enough to leave.

I think the worst part is I want it to hurt.
I want to feel the hitch in my breathing
as we make eye contact in a bustling room.
I want to feel my eyes dim
as I watch you throw your head back in pure bliss.
I want to feel my stomach tugging
at my heart strings to come from its cage
into the chambers of my stomach
as my gut engulfs my heart into a hug.
I want to feel my mouth dry
as my lips slightly part releasing
a wave of sadness through my veins.
I want to feel the world stop around me
but continue to move about
as if my own little world didn't just shatter.
I want to feel small because,
at this rate, none of that hurts at all.

Where are all of these thoughts coming from?
My head had become a stagnant body of water
collecting algae and larvae, but a storm has started inside of me.
The pebbles I call my thoughts swim in the raging currents
and are flowing straight to my hand.

My thoughts run from hot to cold
when they come from my heart to my brain.
I have such a turbulent mind
my winds create a tornado in my brain.
They scatter my thoughts
to the darkest corners of my head
and mix together like the sand on the beach.
I can't let the gust carry me away
or I'll lose my mind.
Maybe that's why I write.
This is my way to control my wind and *vent*.

These poems take time,
but I feel a different passion leading my hand.
I'm writing to learn from myself.
To see if I'm okay because, as humans,
we experience so many emotions a day,
but my hand can spell that out for me
better than the feelings in my head.

I'm tired of
showing my light
to people who like
to sit in the dark.

I lit myself on fire to keep you warm
even when you tried to put me out.
I exhausted and expired, and you sat there.
Your eyes were to the stars and you wondered why
I stopped burning as you set your bucket to the side.

I think what hurt
the most was opening
my favorite novel
and realizing it had lost its luster.
That's how I feel about you.

What I hate the most is that
I built my expectations out of sand.
My structure crumbled
when the sky cried over
my castle.

You told me that my eyes tell a story. That there was something hidden behind them and that there's more to me than what I let on. You often hide from my eyes because you fear I'll see right through you. They're so warm but could be so cold. You said you could see the faces of everyone who had ever hurt me when the sun hit the right spot. For someone so obsessed with my eyes, you sure didn't see your own reflection in them. You're the pain in my eyes that speaks volumes colored with nostalgia. If it wasn't your face you saw, who are the people you blame for my pain?

When we were younger, you had mocked me
for playing with dolls. It's ironic because
that's what you did with people when we were growing up.
You colored my skin, ripped out my hair, disassembled my body.
Then I was tossed aside so you could ruin another as if they were
some carbon copy at your dispense.
You're a child, and I was your toy.

That was the thing about us.
I would think all day and night that you were the toxic one
in the relationship and was able to sleep peacefully.
Now, come to think of it, we were toxic for each other.
Although, I'm not sure if I'm just giving you the benefit of the
doubt like I always did. Some habits don't change.

You are a good memory.
In fact, one of my favorites.
I didn't mean to reminisce
to the point I forgot.

I never thought I was a brooding cloud
and I didn't realize how bad my temper was
until I set a fire with my lightning strike.

I thought I was the breeze that danced with the trees
or the light that peeked
through the branches and scattered on the grass,
but I'm not.

I'm the storm that rains on your parade.
I don't mean to dim
your light with my tears.

I am the cause of your pain
and all the days you felt the rain.

I didn't mean to turn you
into something you're not,
but I'm sure you felt the
same about me.

You gave me a candle
and told me to light it
when I needed you the most.
You said it would represent
the love we shared.
I burned it last night.
It wasn't bright
and you forgot to tell me
candles burn out.

If I could paint with the colors
you make me feel,
my canvas would be saturated with black ink
bleeding from my brush.
I'd be a liar to say your canvas remained white.
If you had a blank canvas
that would mean we would have
somewhere to start.

How twisted is it
that the one person
I wanted to save
is the one I killed?

Our love was purgatory.
Going in seemed normal,
maybe, even fun,
but there were no heavenly aspects of us.
You never let us fly.
You took me to the beach
and threw me in the ocean.
My breath danced with the waves
and I slept with the fishes those cold nights.
You threw me in hell
to secure your spot in heaven
as you praised your
selfish goddess.

Yesterday,
all those days we spent
are going away.
Memories now fading
to grey.

My love became such a normality
like the sun shining during the day.
You only noticed me when the cold front
came upon you.

I gave my heart as a promise.
How naive of me.
I forgot promises can be broken.

You gave me one red balloon for my birthday.
It stayed and floated around my room.
Until, one November night,
I took it outside and let it go.

My thoughts
have walked more steps
than I have taken
in my lifetime.

I still look at our star every night
to fill the void moving away created.
Although, a glance at night
doesn't bring me closer to you.
When I look, I can feel you
 fill the cracks of my heart
with your tears as you stare back.

Handwritten notes, with pen smears and faded tears,
sit in your closet in a box I gave you on the Fourth of July.
Words were spoken but were not appreciated enough.
The words take you back to a small town with small minds,
remembering the girl with the big heart you left behind.
Time collects weight as do the feelings
your heart carries behind your eyes.
You read the scribbles of documented feelings from so long ago
and retreat to the neighborhood your memories play in.
You see your old house with busted windows and wind chimes blowing
in the distance. The room where you had your first kiss and the shower
you hid your tears in. You see your mom in the backyard on the phone
with your father and your dog fumbling around
and pawning for your attention.
You fall into nostalgia only to catch yourself dreaming.
Your mom is gone and so is your father.
Your dog ran away because he couldn't stay any longer.
Your faucet and drain ran out of water
and the girl who loved you, well, who knows where she wandered.
No, you're left with these letters because people have moved on,
but at least you have something to wake up to at dawn.

Your heart can burn from the sun
just as fast as it can freeze from the cold.

Maybe darkness can be brighter than the light.
It's a place in life that can give you the desire to find hope.
Darkness is assumed as evil and hopeless because people wallow.
Wallowing is like complaining that it's too dark when all
you must do is be brave, open your
eyes, and turn on the light.

My handwriting would change when I wrote to you.
It was much clearer and of broad shape.
I'm naturally a very messy and loopy person.
So, why would I change myself so you could understand me?

To fall in love and be vulnerable
isn't stupid, it's courageous.
It's ironic how it takes more love
to pick us up when we fall too hard.

I don't believe in coincidences.
Truth is,
We all meet people on
Purpose.

No one's the victim
because no one is completely
innocent.

I have come to love people
I never thought of loving.
Then I realized,
I shouldn't have to think of loving
it just happens.

You must first
experience
hatred to fully
appreciate
love.

I mistook anxiety for love
realizing all of this awakens my soul.
I feel as free as a dove no longer looking for love
in an abandoned tree I used to call my home.

You can't burn me anymore
with your heart of ice.

I saw
a different girl
that night when
I got out of the shower.
She was a stranger,
yet I understood her so well.

November feelings

What we used to call them

As if they are from some distant time

when things were better,

What about December?

What happened in January?

Did you want to forget about February?

March is still resonating on my lips.

April is still sinking into my heart.

Months bleed together and I'm starting to forget those April showers, but I can't seem to forget what it felt like to stand under the stars. Your jacket over my shoulders.

Why do those moments stay frozen in my mind?

I can't remember the past couple of days,

but I can remember those fleeting minutes.

When we snuck out of the house to dance in the road in December, or when we traded our hearts the night you left.

There's no such thing as November feelings.

They're not in the past.

They've always been on my mind, but not in the ways you think.

The calendar reminds me it's June and while the June bugs dance with the fireflies, I can't help but remember the sound of crunching leaves under my feet as my skin drinks up the sunshine.

Heart breaks
Eyes tear
Hands write
This is who I am.

The freckles on my cheeks are scars
from the tears of broken promises
left over the years from an empty town.

You sat in the living room
as you made your own stars,
they decorated your cheeks
and broke people's hearts.

This rose has never died
just grew from a weeded bed.

Maybe
I was writing about
the wrong person
all along

I thought you should know that the firefighters saved the girl trapped behind the door. The funny thing was the door was unlocked the whole time and she could've escaped. No, she stayed because she was trying to save you. She was crying and screaming. We had to grab her and take her down the stairs before she suffered severe burns. She flailed and tried to escape from our grasp to save you. Why you out of all people? You caused the fire. You're the reason she almost died. She survived with some cuts, bruises, and minor burns. I just thought you should know what you did. She's healed and better than ever.

-Gravestone talk

There's something about him that makes me feel more human. He reminds me I'm not unbreakable, untouchable, unlovable. He awakens my body in ways that remind me that I have a heart and that I can suddenly stop breathing when he's around me. Often, I get so wrapped up in my own thoughts and maintaining others I become numb to my flesh, but I awaken through his song as it sends chills and echoes through my brain.

Through the darkness,
the color found its way back
into my veins.

9:04 PM

At the end of the day,
these brown eyes lose their luster.
She gave her light to the vampires in her memory boxes.
The ones that sucked the love out of her bleeding heart.
She walks through the door and fumbles around on a guitar to
try to remember the words to her soul.
She sits and stares.
Thoughts move like currents washing over her eyes.
Fatigue drowns her body and she gives out.
Her eyes try to swim to the sea of stars.
The clouds fade, the moon shines, and she breathes.
She questions, but can't seem to remember
what she wants the answer to.
Instead, her mind drifts and she looks to the star
the one they named together.
The star kisses her cheeks and gives its life for her light.
The morning comes and the star dies with the night,
but the girl feels her spirit return in hopes to live
like the star does at night.

I've learned that friends don't last
when you're stuck in the past
of what could, what should, and what if
and maybe for a sec
I'll get out of my head
and see the star and the sun share the same sky

You see, I saw you as the sun
and I was just another star
Although, we were in the same place,
I never saw us face to face.
You liked the day
I stayed for the night
Little did I know, you were worth the fight

Because, you see, the sun and the star are the same thing
With them, days and nights bleed together
Old friends, memory trips, it truly couldn't be better,
but you see the dark took over
and the sun stopped shining
leaving the stars at night to stop flying

The sun and her star
the stretch of space is much too far
Little lights burning not too bright
Considering, the two never took flight
One wanted to dance around
the other wanted to be wished on

Again, divided by the day and night
left to think about the lessons
that should have been learned, but here we are again tonight
not shining too bright

I've learned that friends don't last
when you're stuck in the past
of what could, what should, and what if
and maybe for a sec
I'll get out of my head
and see the star and the sun share the same sky yet again

Because the sun is like the star,
just like you and me,
and they found each other
when the sun wished on her brother
to be one of them again.

Look to the stars
because they'll be there for you
when your world is on fire
and your ground is falling apart.

A toast to a new love.
One that will grow through the colors
Of humanity and touch souls.
Bring the broken together and may be reborn
Through their pain.

- *A Prayer for the Romantics*

.

A year of words
Months of tears
Weeks of heartbreak
Days of laughter
Minutes of staring
and, in that moment,
in those seconds,
I felt everything
I had ever written about.

Dear Mom,

Thank you for reminding me of who I am.

You give me the courage to put my heart on the line.

Through all the laughter, heartbreak, and tears you've always managed to help piece me back together. Me and you against the world, remember? It's rather funny that you say I'm the braver more outgoing version of you, yet you're the one that inspired me to be this way. You're selfless, tough, and I can only hope to be like you one day. You made me, but I made this.

This is for you, Mom.

Feel free to vent below

_____
_____
_____
_____
_____
_____
_____
_____
_____
_____
_____
_____
_____
_____
_____
_____
_____
_____
_____
_____
_____
_____
_____
_____
_____
_____
_____
_____
_____
_____
_____
_____
_____
_____
_____

Rosalyn Alexandra, a senior in high school, an artist, musician, and aspiring author/poet takes inspiration from the world around her. She likes to write through the eyes of characters and people in her everyday life. She is a storyteller and strives to reach people through poetry, stories, and songs. During her Sophomore year in high school, she started to become more of an avid writer using her social conflicts and home life as fuel to her hand. It allowed her to sort through her emotions and thoughts and find her true voice. She writes in hopes to encourage and inspire others to not be afraid to be honest with yourself and the world. Now eighteen, she is getting ready to explore the new realm of "adulthood" and plans to write and publish more along the way.

She stresses that "our hearts and minds undergo the elements of emotion every day. Given how fleeting life is, we hardly have time to express what goes on inside. We must learn to let thoughts out and let things go. *Vent* is inspired by the clutter in our heads. Take this book and read the words I've patched together. I hope these words paint parts of your own story and encourages you to tell yours." (Rosalyn Alexandra 2018). She writes in hopes to inspire others to scribble down their thoughts. She would love to hear from you, feel free to share your thoughts. You can contact her via email or on social media. You can also keep up with her on all platforms below. She is currently working on her next project. Stay tuned.

Instagram: @rosiearuiz

Twitter: @rabookthoughts

YouTube: Rosalyn Alexandra

Pinterest: Rosalyn Alexandra

Email: rosalynalexandrapoetry@gmail.com

CPSIA information can be obtained
at www.ICGtesting.com
Printed in the USA
LVHW021015150419
614195LV00015B/499/P